Matthew Gray

COIN COLLECTING

FOR BEGINNERS

A COMPLETE GUIDE TO START YOUR FIRST COIN COLLECTION FOR HOBBY OR BUSINESS AND LEARN HOW TO FIND AND VALUE THE BEST COINS.

Table of Contents

Introduction

Are you new to the world of coins? Perhaps you've been collecting for a while and seek some guidance on which coins to concentrate on next. Either way, this book is here to help! It focuses on everything about getting started, meaningful information about coin collecting, beginner tips for selecting your first coins, and more.

You may have heard the term "coin-collecting" and maybe even wondered what it's all about. Or you have an interest in starting a coin collection for fun. Whatever your case may be, the whole idea of collecting coins may seem very confusing to you.

However!

You need to know that Coins are by far the most popular kind of collectibles. There are several different coins that you can gather, whether you are a person who likes to keep them in little baggies and boxes or one who wants to display them in a case at home or the office.

A coin collection is a hobby in which people collect rare or valuable coins worldwide. Some people enjoy the history behind each coin, while others focus on collecting only physical coins. No matter your reason for getting started, you will enjoy this hobby, especially if you love history or are interested in finance and economics.

Usually, a particular era or coin type should attract you the most. For instance, if you're into American history, you may enjoy collecting coins minted in the colonial times of the United States. Some people like collecting certain coins or commemorative coins usually made out of precious metals and are worth more money than their face value.

Coin collecting can be a fun and enjoyable hobby. However, it is also an investment because it can be a great way to grow your money over time. Once you learn how to buy and sell coins, you will develop your savings over time and begin earning interest. Though this can be challenging if you are new to the hobby, investing in coins will eventually feel more interesting once you read this book.

"Coin Collecting for Beginners: A Complete Guide to Start Your First Coin Collection for Hobby or Business and Learn how to Find and Value the Best Coins"

The book focuses on beginners interested in starting a Coin Collecting journey (either as a business or hobby). It guides you through finding out what fine coin you would like to collect, the best places to look for them, how to store them, and even teaches how to differentiate the real ones from the counterfeit and more.

Coin collecting becomes fun, inexpensive, and relatively easy for any beginner to start with this book. It also offers exclusive ideas that help create and manage a Coin Selling and Investment Business.

Don't delay any longer; read on to learn the several tips you can use when starting a coin-collecting hobby or business.

What is Numismatics?

Numismatics is the study of coins, medals, and tokens.

According to the most widely accepted definition, it is the systematic collection and study of coins. It is characterized as coin collecting in a very narrow sense.

Numismatics usually involves the study of any metal that has been utilized by the human beings of a particular era or time in history.

Numismatists are coin collectors who study the discipline of numismatics. People interested in Ancient Greek or Roman coins, medieval or hammered coins, and current struck coins are typical of this group.

It offers the opportunity of studying the history and the culture of different 3rd world countries. For example, to check the ancient coins found in Anatolia, you should visit

Turkey. To study American coins, you will have to travel to the U.S.A.

You can also get unique gifts for your friends as it's not very expensive. The economic, social, political, cultural, and aesthetic tendencies of the moment are reflected in numismatics. If there is a high demand for them, their intrinsic numismatic value may rise above their current value.

Numismatics allows you to buy coins cheap and sell expensive. If you purchase an ancient coin valued at 10 $, and its price rises, you can sell it off in profit. But if you put that money in the bank, you will never be able to make a profit like this.

It's also a way of investing as it provides outstanding returns compared to any other investment field.

While numismatic materials such as the Ancient Greek or Roman coins, medieval or hammered coins, and current struck coins are primarily valued for economic and commercial value, they also have significant historical and artistic value.

Coins are also essential and valued in archeology because they reflect the people who minted them or the time they were coined.

Numismatics is also expanding very fast as a hobby in the past few years due to the Internet, social networks, and the Internet in general.

Brief History of Coins and Coin Collection

Coins have been around since ancient times, where they were made of precious metals. Today, some coins are still made of precious metal, but modern coins are made mostly of aluminum, copper, or nickel. During ancient times, they were used as the legal means of payment.

The term, Numismatics; coin collecting as we know it, is derived from the Greek word "nomisma," meaning "legal cash or coin." While we now use checks, paper bills, and, increasingly, credit cards for our daily expenditures, ancient societies adapted coins as their payment system.

Lydia in Asia Minor, which is now part of Turkey but was under Greek influence at the time, created the earliest coins known to have been minted. They have a 2,600year-old history. They used Gold and silver alloy to make the first coins.

The Lydians were business-minded people at the time. They could create a prosperous civilization that advanced trade, economy, and commerce. This era's coins demonstrate how coin design has progressed over time.

Gold and silver ingots were the most popular forms of payment during the period. Because there were no standards and many dishonest merchants, each transaction involving gold and silver payment necessitated an accurate weighing of the medium.

Around 650 B.C., coins were invented, and they were struck with standardized gold and silver weights. The government branded it with a value guarantee. The development of coinage as a primary medium of exchange occurred in the next century.

Numismatics or Coin collection is considered to have started with the first coin. Because there were no banks at the time, collecting them seemed like an excellent way to keep them safe. They were being stockpiled for their inherent value as well as their rarity. These coins have been passed down through the generations as a family heirloom.

According to some researchers, actual coin collecting originated in the late Middle Ages, when numerous European kings searched and acquired unique coins used as money by ancient societies. They discovered that no two coins were similar due to the many procedures used to strike the coins. Coins were struck by hand then, and it wasn't until the 1500s that machine-minted coins became popular. This activity is commonly referred to as the "Hobby of Royalty" because it began with European kings collecting coins.

During the Renaissance, coin collecting became popular, and many ambitious individuals began to make a plethora of high-quality counterfeit. Because of their quality, antiquity, and historical significance, even these forgeries have been given a high-value today.

1st Copper Coins

The first copper coins were minted in the United States in 1793 as part of the Coinage Act, and they were made at the Philadelphia Mint. At the time, production was done by hand, and each coin was struck one by one. On March 3, 1835, the government devised a mint marking system to differentiate coins manufactured in each branch.

Rules governed the identification of coins stamped at each unit. They were supposed to ensure that all coinage was under their supervision and that coinage output was uniform across the board.

Countries such as Italy, France, Rome, China, Japan, and Austria all minted coins into circulation during these ancient times.

Modern Numismatics

The study of coins from the mid-seventeenth to the twenty-first century is modern numismatics. Machines first minted coins during this period. Modern numismatics caters to collectors and amateur enthusiasts; still, ancient coins attracted the attention of professional researchers, historians, and archeologists due to their historical and archeological value.

Modern Numismatics is concerned with determining the relative rarity based on its production and use. Coin variants, mint-made errors, the effect of progressive die wear, mint markings, and figures are among the other topics of interest in modern numismatics.

The American Numismatic Society (A.N.S.), an international non-profit organization dedicated to preserving and studying coins and other numismatic artifacts such as medals and paper money, was founded in 1858 by a group of collectors.

Coins with historical significance, mint mistakes, limited editions, and commemorative coins are among the most sought by today's coin collectors. In this regard, learning how to grade coins effectively is one of the most valuable talents a coin collector can have.

How Coins Are Made- The Minting Process

Coins are actually quite simple — they've just stamped metal discs. Yet their simplicity belies a surprisingly complex and well-organized process that takes years and hundreds of people to execute.

If you're new to coin collecting, learning how coins are manufactured will help you grasp the various types of coins available. It will explain why some coins are uncirculated while others are referred to as resistant coins.

Ancient Coins:

Artisans were manufacturing everything from domestic goods to agricultural tools in ancient times. Making coins was one of their responsibilities. They employed minimal instruments, and the outcome was primarily dependent on their abilities. The quality of the struck coins varies, from

Palestine's "widow's mite" to Greek Sicily's exquisite silver pieces.

An oven for heating blanks or "flans," tongs, an anvil situated on a table or bench, and a pair of dies for impressing the design into the flan were the primary instruments used by the artisans. Dies were made of hard bronze or iron. Bronze corroded more quickly than silver, although it was easier to engrave and not tarnish.

The Greeks employed iron dies for their most significant coins, which show indications of rust. The obverse die was put on the anvil, and the reverse die was struck to form the impression.

Modern United States Coins

In the United States, modern-era coins began in the private sector. Some coinage blanks, planchets, and other materials purchased by the U.S. Mint were made by private enterprises. In 1792, the U.S. Congress passed the Coinage Act, which established the United States Mint as part of the U.S. Treasury Department. Many foreign and colonial currencies were used before it.

The new law mandated the establishment of a national mint in Philadelphia, the nation's capital at the time. The United States Mint is in charge of producing, selling, and safeguarding the country's currency and assets. Between 14 and 28 billion circulation coins are produced annually, and 65 to 80 million coins are minted every day as of 2004. Only coins produced by the United States Mint are accepted as legal money in the United States.

All materials needed to make U.S. coins are purchased from commercial suppliers. The U.S. Mint receives pre-made one-cent coin blanks but creates five-cent coin blanks and cupronickel clad coins from the strip.

The production procedure is essentially the same for all denominations. Dimes, quarters, half dollars, and dollars, on the other hand, go through a process known as "reeding," which leaves microscopic ridges on the coins. These ridges prevent the precious metal in gold and silver coins from being illegally shaved or clipped. It may no longer be essential, but it is being done to honor a long-standing procedure extending back to colonial times. It's also to aid visually impaired people in recognizing the coins.

All circulating coins must bear the inscriptions "Liberty," "In God We Trust," "The United States of America," and "E Pluribus Unum," as well as the denomination and year of issuance, as required by law. Since 1909, the slogan "In God We Trust" has been on the one-cent currency, and since 1916, on the ten-cent denomination. All gold and silver dollar coins, half-dollar coins, and quarter coins began to feature this inscription on July 1, 1908.

Minting Process

Minting is the process deemed as adding a new coin to circulation or changing the function of an existing coin. Minting coins follows a delicate process which is:

Blanking:

To make the nickel, dime, quarter, half-dollar, and the dollar, the U.S. Mint purchases strips of metal that are 13 inches broad and 1,500 feet long. The strips come in a coil form. Each coil is passed into a blanking press, which punches out blanks, which are spherical discs. Webbing, the leftover strip, is sliced and recycled. (After supplying fabricators with copper and zinc, the Mint purchases ready-to-stamp blanks for the cent.)

Blanks are planchets that have not undergone the required processing processes before being struck into coins. A planchet is a blank that has completed all the necessary procedures and is ready to be pounded. These blanks are often larger than completed coins. They feature burrs on the edges, which are eliminated during the subsequent operations.

Annealing, washing, and drying:

To soften the blanks, they are heated in an annealing furnace. After that, they're put through a washing machine and dryer.

The blanks harden as a result of the finish rolling and blanking activities. They're cooked to around 1400 degrees Fahrenheit in a controlled environment. The annealing process relaxes the crystal structure of the materials, making them easier to work on. The life of the coining dies extended due to the lower striking pressure.

On the blanks, the annealing process generates minor discoloration. The blanks are thrown against one other and sent through a chemical bath to remove them. The blanks are then dried with pressurized hot air, and if necessary, parts of them are transferred to the upsetting mill.

Ridding:

Ridding is the third step. The blanks are screened on "riddles" before being upset to remove the wrong size or form.

Upsetting:

The suitable blanks are then run through an upsetting mill. A rim forms around their edges as a result of this.

The upsetting mill consists of a revolving wheel with a groove on one edge that fits into a curving segment with its own track. The raised rim created during the process sizes and forms the blank, allowing it to feed more easily through the press and hardening the edge, preventing metal from escaping between the obverse die and the collar.

Striking:

The blanks are then sent to the coining press. They are then stamped with the designs and inscriptions that identify them as authentic U.S. coins.

Inspecting:

Each batch of newly struck coins is spot-checked by press operators using magnifying lenses.

Bagging and Counting:

Finally, the coins are counted and deposited into huge bags using an automatic counting system. The bags are sealed, placed onto pallets, and transported to the vaults for storage. Trucks deliver new coinage to Federal Reserve Banks. The coins are then delivered to your local bank!

Coin Distribution

The United States Mint is constantly improving its methods for estimating coinage demand. This is to ensure that the movement of U.S. coinage is efficient and steady. The U.S. Mint plans production and coin distribution schedules using economic factors and historical seasonal trends. It's also used to calculate data related to coin production and distribution.

Because forecasting isn't always correct, production must account for potential deviations. The coins are usually transported in armored tractor-trailer trucks.

How are the coins distributed?

The distribution of coins in the U.S. is done through the Bureau of Engraving and Printing. They work with a schedule to produce coins when they are needed. The plan is based on the demand for coins by the public and businesses.

The Basics of Coin Collecting

Coin collecting is an enjoyable hobby with a thriving community of collectors worldwide. Coins come in all shapes and sizes, with wide-ranging interests from different Collectors.

Coin collecting can be a fun and profitable pastime. There's something perpetually beautiful about a piece of cash that is assessed at (often considerably) more than its original value and also bears the history of its time.

Coins often depict royalty, great leaders, history, power, and patriotism. For example, ancient coins depicted Julius Caesar and Alexander the Great; modern coins depict Henry VIII, Napoleon, George Washington, and Abraham Lincoln.

Coin collecting can be done by anyone, regardless of age or experience. However, most collectors start young. As kids learn about the history of coins, they often notice how much money there is in the world. Many children also are interested in finding new things, such as lost treasure.

Other people start collecting coins after discovering an intriguing coin in their change, inheriting a coin collection, or getting a few coins through other methods. Others believe they have found a rare and valuable coin and hope to make a quick buck.

When you start at first, Coin collecting can be a perplexing hobby, especially when there appears to be so much to learn about it.

How do you get started, and where do you go from there?

In this chapter, I've gathered some of the most fundamental aspects of coin collecting: the must-haves to begin with, as well as the foundation rules upon which you should grow your collection. We'll cover some basic concepts, like what coins are and how they're made.

I will also discuss where to find different types of coins and some potential pitfalls if you decide to start collecting. It's time for your million-dollar idea!

Coin Collection: The Art, the Business and the Science

The pleasure and reward of coin collecting are different from other hobbies such as stamping or paper money. Coin collecting has a rich history and can be valuable to the serious collector.

The hobby or business of Coin Collecting requires patience, knowledge, and a deep understanding of the coins you collect. Most coin collectors are passionate about the history, rarity, and type of coins they collect.

For instance, the first Flowing Hair Silver Dollar was minted in 1794 and is currently valued at $10 million. And this isn't an isolated incident. People have made fortunes off of pennies over the years. As a result, it's simple to see why so many people are interested in coin collecting and what it entails.

However, coin collecting is much more than that. It is an art—just as collecting art is an act of creativity in and of itself (if that makes any sense).

Coin collecting is also fascinating from a scientific and historical standpoint. Everyone should be aware of specific "technicalities" before beginning to collect money, as you will see throughout this book. But don't worry; these technicalities will be interesting, I promise.

Coin collecting began as a seemingly natural and reasonable behavior: people saved their high-value coins (such as those made of silver or gold) and spent their lower-value ones. People began to acquire coins for their aesthetic appeal as well over time. For example, many individuals became interested in old Roman coins during the Renaissance (which also attracted a lot of forgeries into the "industry").

The 1893 World Columbian Exposition, which also featured a commemorative U.S. dollar coin, heralded the birth of contemporary coin collecting. Coin collecting has risen in popularity throughout the twentieth century, with a sharp surge in interest in the last three decades.

Refined gentlemen in Victorian times took satisfaction in collecting at least a small collection of antiques (which frequently included coins as well). The activity was already well-known and popular, so it was only a matter of time before it attracted additional devotees.

The number of coin collectors in the United States is unknown (or the world, really). However, some estimates suggest that as many as ten million people are engaged in coin collecting (only in the U.S.).

On the other hand, Coin collecting should not be considered a get-rich-quick scam in any way. Yes, coin collections can make you a lot of money, but the truth is that those rare finds need significant investment and a lot of work.

Before you even start learning about the subtleties of coin collecting, make sure you're familiar with the two primary types of people who are interested in it.

All Coin collectors fall under the first type. These collect various coins and sort them into categories based on their preferences. For instance: era, presidents, country, etc.

Numismatic specialists fall into the second type. The most significant difference between them and the previous group, Coin Collectors, is that they approach coin collecting more methodically. They can assess a coin, confirm its validity, and trace its history, manufacturing, and materials back to its very origins.

In addition, numismatics is a field that encompasses coin science and research and the study of everything that can be used as a kind of currency, such as token bills, medals, and tokens.

Although all numismatists are coin collectors in some ways, not all coin collectors are numismatists.

Furthermore, while coin collectors form clubs, numismatists are more likely to be linked with official institutions that focus on their field of study.

Here are a few of the most well-known numismatists' organizations from throughout the world:

- The Czech Numismatic Society, a non-profit organization dedicated to studying coins.

- The Guild of Ancient Coin Collectors

- The Royal Numismatic Society, a numismatic society based in the United Kingdom.

- America's Archeological Institute

Also, as you might expect, several of these organizations place a premium on the location of their members or headquarters. On the other hand, others are laser-focused on a particular area of interest.

Who Collects Coins?

What may be an even more essential fallacy to debunk is the definition of a coin collector? Coin collecting is often linked with the wealthy, maybe because of the image of Victorian gentlemen interested in antiques.

That isn't always the case, though.

Coin collecting is now a hobby that appeals to various socioeconomic classes, ages, and general interests. Everyone these days can be a coin collector, from youngsters to grandparents, engineers to artists, and men to women.

Who is it that gathers coins today?

Any of the following classes could be the case:

A classic hunter will usually go out hunting with a list and make sure he sticks to it. The collector is well-organized and consistent, and they will often not stop until they have checked off all of the items or coins on their to-do list.

The aesthetic collector is primarily interested in coins that have a pleasing appearance. The appearance of these coins is sometimes more significant to this type of collector than their evaluated value.

A speculator will only collect to increase the value of his investment. As a general rule, I would not advise you to do this, especially as a beginner. Coin collecting can be about much more than just profit.

The perfectionist will never stop looking for flawless coins in every way. They want the coin to appear faultless, to be precious, and to be in excellent shape.

The bargain or cheap collector will want to acquire as much as possible and always look for a good deal. His primary consideration is affordability, and he will hoard coins just because they are very inexpensive.

The presenter is the type of collector that does things like this to brag about his collection. In his home, he will create a complete altar for his coins, and he will not miss an occasion to show them off to anybody he brings over.

Sometimes, the academic collector is also a numismatist (at least at the amateur level). He'll amass not only coins but also a wealth of information about them, to the point that he'll be able to create a book on the subject.

Historian collectors will collect coins since they are historical artifacts. Coins are living testaments to a bygone era. This type of collector will have an almost emotional bond with his coins.

The patriot will mainly collect coins related to his country's past. Most of the time, the same person would also collect other artifacts relating to his homeland.

Of course, you may develop into a collector who does not fit neatly into any of the groups mentioned above. The point of discussing them was not to help you "choose" a typology but to show you that there are many different types of coin collectors. This is a hobby that almost everyone can enjoy.

Kind Of Coins

There are a few things to keep in mind when starting a coin collection. Of course, you are free to proceed in any way you see fit. Finally, coin collecting should be a hobby—yet, as we all know, hobbies aren't usually neatly arranged and labeled.

Suppose you want to get out on the right foot and make collecting valuable coins in several verticals easier in the future. In that case, you should follow the suggestions in this chapter. Hopefully, at the end of it, you'll have learned everything there is to know about prepping for your foray into the valuable world of coin collecting.

Different Kinds of Coins

Coins come in many different shapes and sizes, including round and square. They also feature different colors on their surfaces, such as gold and silver.

Different criteria can be used to classify coins (such as the material used for making them, for example, or the event on which they were created). To make things easier for you, we won't go into too much detail about the specific categories. Instead, we will present you with the most common coin types and terms in general.

Gold and Silver Coin:

Since ancient times, most countries have used gold and silver coins. These countries include Ancient Rome, Ancient Greece, Egypt, England, and the United States.

Gold Coins:

Gold Coins are pretty awesome. They're worth more than any other metal, they're used to store wealth, and they're just cool looking.

Gold doesn't exist in its pure form. With usual mining techniques, it's not possible to find enough for what would be considered a significant amount of gold because it's so rare. That's why most gold is located in the ground in the veins of other minerals.

These veins are deep inside the Earth, thousands of feet down. The rock from which these tiny veins are formed is called quartz, and it's loaded with gold. The gold itself is mixed with other metals and minerals surrounding it. These additional minerals include iron, copper, silver, and certain types of precious stones like diamonds (although diamonds and quartz tend to stick together as they're close relatives).

Gold has always been a desirable investment, and now that the price of gold is at all-time highs, it is much more so. When people think of gold, they usually think of bars. Still, gold coins have other advantages, such as economic viability and modest denominations.

Silver Coin:

Silver coins can be used as a medium of exchange. Still, they are more often used as a store of value due to their inherent rarity relative to paper money or other metals such as gold.

Silver coins are more prevalent in countries where their circulation is legal. They are widely considered to exhibit higher value than other coins with similar or lesser usage. They also have an essential role in commerce and a minor form of physical currency. In some cases, silver is minted for coinage.

Coins usually produced for this purpose are 90% pure ("bullion") silver or 90% base material with no other elements (such as copper) included improving the appearance of the coin. However, there are some cases where silver coins were struck to higher purity standards.

Gold and silver coins are no longer used in regular transactions, but collectors highly seek them. Depending on what type of gold or silver coin you're looking for, the cost of such a piece can be relatively high.

Commemorative Coins

Commemorative coins feature a design on one side to commemorate a person, event, or cause that's significant to a particular nation or region. They serve as a souvenir and tangible reminder of the importance of the occasion being celebrated.

The use of commemorative coins dates back to ancient times. The ancient Greeks and Romans used coins with images of the emperors and critical historical events, including battles and gladiators' battles. Today, commemorative coins are limited to only the Greeks and Romans. Still, most cultures around the world have unique designs.

The first wave of commemorative coins drew many individuals into coin collecting, and they continue to do so today. Commemorative coins are appealing and elegant to coin collectors and people who aren't interested in coin collecting in general.

Revolutionary Coins:

Revolutionary coins, in a nutshell, are coins that circulated during times of revolution (such as the American Revolution of 1776, for example). These coins can be precious due to their historical significance (but this depends on other factors).

Ancient Coins:

In the present day, coins are a common currency used by many countries worldwide. But while they may not be ancient in form, they have an exciting history that dates back to some of the earliest civilizations in existence, like those found in ancient Mesopotamia or Egypt.

Ancient coins are frequently confused with gold and silver coinage. However, this isn't always the case, as miners utilized different materials to make coins in the past (such as glass, ivory, or porcelain, for example).

Another common misunderstanding regarding ancient coins is that they are prohibitively pricey. While this may be true in some cases, you can still own one (or more) without breaking the bank because a coin's market value is not only influenced by its age.

Another common misunderstanding regarding ancient coins is that they are prohibitively pricey. However, while this may be true in some cases, you can still own one (or more) without breaking the bank because a coin's market value is not only influenced by its age.

Souvenir Pennies:

These coins have a lot of potentials. They're regular coins that have been pressed, stretched, and altered somehow. The most intriguing detail about them is that mutilating coins to put them back into circulation is banned except for these souvenir pennies. Souvenir Pennies make a fun addition to any collector's collection!

Medallions:

The term "medallion" is often used to denote a wide range of coins (including commemorative coins). In general, "medallions" refer to any round, ornamented piece of metal with some importance associated with it (such as monetary value, for example). On the other hand, actual medallions are rarely accompanied by legal tender.

Coin medallions are popular among collectors, jewelers, and those interested in numismatics because they can be precious. However, it would help if you looked beyond the value of a coin medallion. Overall quality should be your primary consideration when purchasing one of these coins.

Tokens

Trade tokens are scarce and valuable collectibles. They can be worth several hundreds of dollars in some cases (e.g., Civil War tokens, for example). Typically, these tokens were made during financial hardship when silver and gold were rare. However, People still required a form of payment.

Tokens were often for $1 or less at face value, although some tokens can be worth as much as $5. They were utilized in ordinary transactions just like "standard" circulation coins.

The specialty of coin tokens is that they need not be redeemed immediately or within any specific period. Coin tokens can be traded only with other investors who hold them as non-redeemable stock or cash. This means that they can be separated from each other.

Error Coins:

They occur when there is an error in producing these coins (such as a double denomination, over the date, or brokerage). They came out of the mint in this condition, and some may be persuaded to believe they are worthless. On the other hand, error coins can be pretty expensive depending on the flaw and their era.

Error coins, in general, can be defined as a coin that is in some way defective. Whether the error in the coin is caused by damage or tooling, or design faults, it will affect its value.

Types of Errors in coins include:

- Dies - coins struck on the wrong planchet or planchets that don't match dies.

- Hammering - where a coin's die is damaged either by tooling or during the coin's production.

- Striking - where there are issues with a coin's striking.

- Clashing - where there has been an issue with how two dies have been used together to make a milled coin.

B.U. Rolls:

B.U. Rolls are emblematic of the new generation of coin collectors that emerged at the end of the 1950s and 1960s. These "rolls" were bank-wrapped Brilliant Uncirculated little stashes of coins that drove collectors insane throughout the period. Collectors learned that, even though some of these B.U.Rolls were represented as rare, they were relatively common, and their 15-minute glory began to wane (as the millions had manufactured them). As a result, B.U. Rolls are often startlingly low in price these days, so you may want to avoid falling into a trap with them.

Silver Certificates:

Silver certificates are a type of obligation backed by the United States government. People utilized old Silver Certificates to exchange one silver dollar. These certificates, however, were only valid until 1964, when the government stopped producing them. For a time, though, customers could exchange their silver certificates for a certain amount of silver, which spawned a whole new coin collecting mania.

Because mintages were initially limited, art bars were highly sought after. However, the market became saturated with these art bars, and customers finally became tired of them.

Art Bars:

These are thin, rectangular silver bars weighing one ounce, having different commemorative designs and a shiny polished surface. They were trendy back in the 1970s.

Because mintages were initially limited, art bars were highly sought after. However, the market became saturated with these art bars, and customers finally became tired of them.

Altogether, there is no such thing as a "proper" or "wrong" coin to collect. Sure, some coins have more worth now than others, but at the end of the day, the value is determined by many things, not just the type of coin.

What Makes Coins Valuable?

Coins have been making their way around civilization for thousands of years now, and the concept of money has changed more than once in that time. However, no matter how much the value of coins changes and how many times they go through or come up with a new concept of money, they remain the most valuable thing people can use in exchange for goods and services.

However, to understand why these coins are worth so much, you must first look into the characteristics which make them valuable.

Characteristics of Coins to Consider

Name of the denomination: Different denominations are issued by each currency (such as the penny, the nickel, the dime, and the quarter, for example).

Type: This does not always apply to the coin types detailed in the previous section of our book but rather to the designs available for each denomination. Coins must be identified by their design and not easily mistaken for any other coin type.

Issue date: Some individuals prefer to collect coins based on the date they were released, which is entirely OK. For example, you might desire to collect all sorts of nickels minted between 1900 to the present.

Year: This collection form contains all coins released during your birth year.

Coins with the same date and mintmark: You might want to collect coins with the same date and mintmark. Keep in mind that this can be more expensive than simply ordering them according to their era, as most coin series feature a very valuable mintmark.

Based on these features, what makes these coins as valuable are:

- The weight standard for the entire coin denomination.
- The content and value of the metal used on the coin.
- How often were the coins minted, and how many pieces were stamped that year.

A coin's legal tender status.

All of these may seem confusing if you are just getting started with your coin collecting. But don't worry; if you are curious and study as much as you can on the subject, you will learn everything there is to know about this lucrative pastime in this book.

The Vocabulary of Coin Collecting

The coin collection has its lingo. While this isn't a full list of every coin collecting term you'll come across, it does contain meanings for the most widely used terms.

Alloy

Cupro-nickel or cupro-zinc coins have a mixture of two or more metals.

Ancient

Any coin struck before 500 A.D. is referred to as a "pre-500" coin.

Bag Marks

Nicks, scuffs, and scratches caused by coins colliding in a mint bag.

Bi-Metallic Coin

A coin with a single metal in the center and a different metal in the outer half.

Blank

A piece of spherical metal intended to be minted into currency later.

Bullion

Bullion is gold or other precious metal coins with little numismatic worth other than the current value of the metal it is comprised of.

Cameo

A coin that has a frosty appearance.

Circulated Coin

A coin that has been used as currency and has some wear.

Commemorative Coin

A coin featuring a design commemorating a historical or present event, a well-known figure, or a significant anniversary.

Error Coin

A coin that has been produced mistakenly or with a different design than intended.

Grade

A prescribed methodology determines a coin's condition.

High Points

the highest point of a coin's design, where the first traces of wear and tear are usually visible.

Legend

The words are engraved around the outside edge; the legend inscription on U.S. coins is E Pluribus Unum.

Mintage

The total number of coins produced by a mint in a given denomination, date, and/or type.

Mint Mark

A sign that identifies the mint that created the coin.

Mint State

An uncirculated coin in perfect condition, with no traces of wear as when it was produced.

Numismatics

The study of coins, paper money, tokens, medals, and other items of a similar nature.

Obverse

A portrait of a president, king, queen, or other national leader appears on the "heads" side of the coin.

Proof Coins

Coins struck with greater pressure than usual using specially polished dies to produce a more highly polished or mirror-like design

Reverse

The back or "tails" side of a coin, the opposite side of the obverse side of a coin.

Rim

The rim of a coin.

Un-circulated coin

A coin that has never been used as money and has no obvious signs of wear.

Variety

Any modification in the design of a coin results in the creation of a new coin type.

We will attempt to define additional terminologies as they appear in this book, but this is a decent starting point for the newbie collector.

Handling and Cleaning Your Coins

Handling

In general, collector coins should be handled with care to avoid wear or the introduction of substances that could cause spots or color changes. Many holders will give ample protection for normal handling but think twice before removing a coin from its holder.

Only the edge of an uncirculated or proof coin should be touched. Fingerprints alone have the potential to lower the coin's grade and, as a result, its value. When inspecting another person's coins, you must always handle them on edge regardless of grade. If you get into the practice of picking up collectible coins by their edges, it will become second nature.

Holding numismatic objects in front of your mouth is not a good idea. Little particles of moisture can cause spots.

Place a coin on a clean, soft surface when placing it down outside a holder. A velvet pad is a perfect surface for handling valuable materials regularly. A clean, soft cloth or blank piece of paper may suffice for less valued things. No coins should be dragged across any surfaces.

Wearing a clean white cloth or surgical gloves and a mask may be necessary if you are handling highly costly coins or many uncirculated or higher grade circulated coins.

Cleaning Coins

In most circumstances, it is not necessary to clean coins. While you might assume that bright coins seem better, collectors prefer coins with their original appearance. Cleaning a coin can halve or perhaps more than halve its collector value.

Like overhauling works of art, cleaning coins is best left to professionals who have the knowledge and experience to determine when it's appropriate, which techniques will work best, and how to employ them effectively.

Suppose you decide to go to the trouble, never clean coins with abrasive cleaners. Even scrubbing the coin with a delicate cloth can leave little but noticeable scratches, lowering the coin's value.

It is better to leave a coin alone if the surface appears to be tarnished. A natural process known to collectors as toning is responsible for the color shift. Chemical reactions have occurred on the coin's surface, most commonly with sulfur compounds. It is not possible to reverse the reaction.

There are "dips" available, which remove molecules off the surface. Dipping is the ideal example of a procedure that, if utilized at all, should only be done by professionals. Natural toning can also boost a coin's worth.

Dirt and other foreign substances stuck to a coin can be removed in some cases. You can soak the coin in olive oil or soapy water for a few days, then rinse it thoroughly with tap water. Allow the coin to air dry or use compressed air to dry it. The coin should not be rubbed. Commercial coin cleaners can also be used to release foreign substances more quickly.

Hairlines will appear on a coin that has been cleaned using an abrasive. Abrasive cleaning can also leave some debris in the coin's crevices.

It may or may not be detectable if the coin has been dipped. It's possible that an original coin exists, although it's improbable. Dipping can also remove the shine from the coin.

A natural coin has a distinct look that reflects its storage history. The toning of haphazardly stored coins has a "dirty" appearance. Coins that have been in a coin cabinet for a long time usually exhibit stunning colored toning.

Coins kept in a clean metal vault (such as an old-style "piggy" bank) can last a long time and remain white (or red). Coins in albums either develop "ring toning" or "one-sided toning," which is far less appealing. Coins kept in mint bags frequently exhibit amazing rainbow toning, comparable to that found in coin cabinets.

Coins made of copper, bronze, or brass that have been cleaned have an artificial tint, resembling a toned gold coin. Even after they've been re-toned, they're still uneven and have an unusual color. The presence of red in the recesses of that V.F. copper coin is not a positive indicator. The copper that has been naturally toned and *circulated* has a pretty uniform color. However, it may be dark and dusty around the lettering and other protected places. Uncirculated copper (particularly proofs) can have an uneven tone, so don't dismiss such a coin automatically.

Silver coins that have been cleaned and re-toned, on the other hand, tend to be extremely consistent in color, including the tops of the inscriptions and protected areas. Silver coins with natural toning will normally display some color variation at these locations. Be aware that a uniform slate grey hue can be easily achieved on silver using a variety of chemicals. Finally, a heavily toned and then dipped silver coin will have a grey look induced by surface roughness rather than tarnish. A close examination with a bright magnifier can reveal this.

According to the ANA, rapid "hardline" color changes do not occur on naturally toned coins. Coins that have been naturally toned show a gradual change in hue or shade. In any case, it's primarily a case of examining a large number of coins and establishing your conclusions. If you're buying coins for your collection, your viewpoint is the most important factor to consider.

How to Handle Coins

A cardinal rule for all coin collectors is to avoid causing wear or introducing any substances that may cause spots or color changes. Try to avoid any direct manual contact with your coins. This means not using your bare hands to handle the coins. Fingerprints are collectible coin's sworn enemies. It is also important to make sure that you do not let one coin touch another coin because it can result in nicks and scratches. To avoid ruining them, remove coins from their storage containers only when absolutely needed and necessary.

Uncirculated or Proof coins should not be handled anywhere but the edge, as even a slight fingerprint may reduce its grade and, thus, its value. Proof coins are struck two or more times with polished dyes on an equally polished planchet; they are legal tender like regular coins.

Uncirculated mint sets are coins packaged by the U.S. government for sale to coin collectors. It is best if you make it a habit to pick up collectible coins by their edges while wearing clean white cotton or surgical gloves. A face mask is also preferable to prevent small particles of moisture that may cause unwanted spots. Never sneeze or cough near coins because this can actually leave marks and ruin the coin.

Mint Coins

Coin holders provide enough protection for ordinary handling. If you must take the coin out and need to put it down outside the holder, make sure you place it on a clean and soft surface, preferably a velvet pad. It is an ideal surface and a must-have for handling valuable numismatic materials. For coins with lesser value, a clean, soft cloth may be used. Avoid dragging coins on any surface to avoid scratches. Take note that even wiping with a soft cloth can cause scratches that reduce its value.

You need to observe several rules when considering cleaning the coins you have just obtained, found, bought or inherited.

1.   Never clean a coin that you do not know the numismatic value of. If you doubt if it's valuable or not, then don't clean it either. It is best to leave coins the way

you found them, untouched. Erring on the conservative side is preferable to ruining the coin for nothing. Store them in holders made for the purpose. Coin collectors and dealers prefer coins in their original condition to not alter their state. Cleaning will probably do more harm than good.

2.   Because you are not supposed to clean the coins yourself, then you need to take the coins to a professional coin cleaning service. They use a technique called "dipping" that will properly clean the coins without reducing their value. This is important especially if the coin's date and details cannot be determined because of corrosion. A professional will know how to avoid or minimize further damage to the coin.

3.   In the situation that you must clean the coin you have discovered, then do it with the least harmful method. Do not use harsh chemicals, sulfuric acid, polishing cloth,

vinegar, abrasive pastes, or devices that give the coin a smooth and shiny result. Experiment first with lesser value coins before coins with high value.

Cleaning is a big issue in coin collecting, so you have to disclose this fact to a buyer if you are selling a coin that you know has been cleaned.

Soaking coin

Cleaning Different Types of Coins

Uncirculated coins – should never be cleaned at all because cleaning will ruin any mint luster.

Gold Coins – should be washed carefully in clean, warm soapy distilled water using a fluffy cotton washcloth or a very soft toothbrush. Gold is a soft metal, so you should take extra care to avoid disfiguring or scratching.

Martha Washington Gold Coin

Silver Coins – valuable silver coins should not be cleaned at all. The blue-green or violet oil-like tarnish, dirt, minerals, or some silver coins' residue have enhanced their appearance and should be left alone. Dark silver coins must be cleaned with ammonia, rubbing alcohol, vinegar, or polish remover with acetone. Do not rub or polish them.

Copper Coins – clean them and soak them in grape oil. If not available, olive oil will do. Never attempt to rub them in any way. However, getting results may take several weeks to a year, so be patient.

Nickel Coins – best cleaned with warm, soapy distilled water using a soft toothbrush. If cleaning badly stained nickel coins, use ammonia diluted 3 to 1 with distilled water.

How to Store Your Coins

It would help if you stored your coins properly to avoid giving them any scratch to reduce their numismatic value. You need to use the proper type of holder depending on the value of the coin you are storing.

There are folders and albums available commercially that you can purchase for storing your series or type collection. When using paper envelopes, make sure that their materials are especially suited for holding coins, especially the high-value ones, since sulfur or other chemicals present in the paper can cause a reaction and change the coin's color.

Plastic flips made of Mylar and acetate are suitable materials for long-term storage, but since they are hard and brittle, they may scratch the coin if the coins are not inserted and removed carefully. "Soft" flips used to be made from polyvinyl chloride (P.V.C.), which decomposed over time and gave disastrous results for the coins. P.V.C. lent a green appearance on the coins. P.V.C. flips are no longer produced and sold in the U.S.

Tubes can hold several same-size coins and are suitable for bulk storage of circulated and higher-grade coins if they are not moved. For more valuable coins, use hard plastic holders as they do not contain harmful materials and can protect coins against scratches and other physical damage.

Collectible Coins in their Cases.

You can opt to use slabs for more valuable coins as they offer good protection. Slabs are hermetically sealed hard plastic holders for individual coins.   One drawback, however, is the expense involved, and you will not be able to get at the coin easily if there is a need to do so.

A dry environment without significant temperature fluctuation and low humidity are important for long-term storage. It would help minimize exposure to moist air as this will cause oxidation. It may not reduce the coin's value, but reducing oxidation will help the coin look more attractive. You need to lace silica gel packets in the coin storage area to control atmospheric moisture. You still need to check on your collection periodically, even if you store them in a safety deposit box. If not stored properly, problems could develop, and you can do something about it before any serious damage occurs.

Grading

Grade refers to the condition of a coin. The primary objective of grading coins is to establish if the coin is "mint state (M.S.) or if it is circulated. There are three basic areas to consider when it comes to coin grading;

Quality of coin die and striking characteristics (fullness of the strike).

The strike of a coin refers to stamping a design into a planchet. The strike can be either strong or weak, and much of this depends on how the coin was designed.

Condition and characteristics of the planchet (luster or brilliance)

Luster is important in establishing the fact of a coin is uncirculated or not. A mint state coin should be free of wear and should not possess any major break in its luster. A circulated coin will manifest a greater quantity of breaks in the luster and, therefore, show a smaller amount of luster.

Amount and type of wear, damage, and the overall eye appeal of the coin.

The fullness of the strike and luster of a coin form an overall quality that is referred to as "eye appeal." A coin can be described as having a good eye appeal because it is strong in one area but can be simply good in another. A coin may be negative in one area but acceptable in another and can still be noted as having below-average eye appeal. Although eye appeal is subjective, most coin collectors will agree that a certain coin has good or bad eye appeal.

If you want to be a good coin collector, you need to master this skill. You can develop this skill through interaction with other experienced collectors, reliable and honest dealers and consulting grading guides. And as with any skill, lots of practice will give you opportunities to improve. Having a good eye will help a lot too.

Grading a coin is considered an art. It is supposed to consider the objective and subjective views that a coin expert has when examining a particular coin. One can objectively determine whether a coin has been worn or not, but how much or to what extent it has affected the coin's overall condition is harder to determine.

Not all experts will agree to a single assessment - that a coin's surface is of such state, or the quality of the luster is this high, or the fullness of the strike is this remarkable. Added to the mix is how these factors affect and interact. A coin may receive a grade saying it has "great eye appeal" or another "superb eye appeal." In common usage, superb may not be interchangeable, but its shade of meaning is barely indistinguishable from each other. This may be different when applied to coin grading?

Grading has a set standard. Coin conditions vary from the poorest state to the best state. A coin in poor condition will have neither the date nor designs discernible, whereas a coin in the best state bears designs which are clear and detailed as if they were just stuck at the mint.

However, since experts are vulnerable to subjectivity, there are varying grades that could be assigned to a coin, depending on how the expert views it. Thus, any coin can receive as many grades as the experts who examined it. This doesn't undermine the expert's opinion, though. It just shows how different people can appreciate a coin.

Being able to form your own assessment of a coin's grade then is important. As the first skill in coin collection, you should be able to determine whether a coin is mint state; that is, it has no visible signs of wear on any of its surface; or circulated, meaning it bears marks of surface wear because of handling.

Before the 1940s, using adjectives was the only way to describe a coin's grade. The numerical grading system in current use was invented by Dr. William Sheldon in that decade. The circulated coin grades were assigned numbers from 1 to 59, while numbers 60 to 70 were used for the mint state coins. 0 is the least desirable, and 70 is a coin in a perfect state. This standard, however, is applicable to U.S. coins only. An abbreviation for an adjective is appended to the number for clarity.

Using adjectives to grade coins was a very subjective and troublesome system since a V.F. for one expert can be an E.F. for another. In fact, coin dealers have often been accused of over-grading a coin in order to get a better price for their merchandise. The addition of the relative numerical precision of the Sheldon scale has helped to make a standardized adjectival grading.

Sheldon's numerical system is now used by most coin collectors and dealers. The following are based on the Official A.N.A. Grading Standards for United States Coin:

aG-3

About Good

G-4

Good

VG-8

Very Good

VG-10

Very Good Plus

F-12

Fine

F-15

Fine Plus

VF-20

Very Fine

VF-30

Very Fine Plus

EF-40

Extremely Fine

EF-45

Choice Extremely Fine

AU-50

About Uncirculated

AU-55

Choice About Uncirculated

AU-58

Very Choice About Uncirculated

Adjectival grades are the most subjective coin grades used before the adoption of the Sheldon 70-point coin grading scale. The following are some of the most common adjectival grades used before the 1940s:

• Poor (P)

• Fair (F.R.)

• About Good (aG)

• Good (G)

• Very Good (V.G.)

• About Fine (aF)

• Fine (F)

• Very Fine (V.F.)

• Good Very Fine (gVF)

• About Extremely Fine (aEF)

• Extremely Fine (E.F.)

- Choice Extremely Fine (X.F.)

- About Uncirculated (A.U.)

- Uncirculated (Unc)

The following are approximately equivalent overall, but they could have had a higher or lower denotation to a particular dealer.

- Brilliant Uncirculated (B.U.)

- Choice Uncirculated (Choice Unc or Choice B.U.)

- Gem Brilliant Uncirculated (Gem B.U.)

A. Uncirculated Coins

Uncirculated coins, also known as a mint state (M.S.), are coins with no wear at all. These coins were never placed in circulation to be used as tender. Their grades are expressed as MS-60 to MS 70. M.S. coins are graded for their luster, the amount, size, and location of contact marks; the amount, size, and location of any hairlines and the quality of the strike, and overall eye beauty. Most numismatics admit that MS 70, a flawless condition of a coin, is an unreachable grade.

An uncirculated coin can have some tarnish, spotting, or discoloration but can still be uncirculated. Therefore, the numismatic value and the market value for many uncirculated coins differ substantially from one grade to another. A grade expressed with an adjective or a number is, at best, a particular opinion of one expert. As mentioned before, you should learn to make your own assessment of a coin's grade be wary of those opinions by others.

B. Circulated Coins

The first thing to look for in grading circulated coins is the extent of the wear it exhibits. But there are other factors to look into, such as the fullness of the strike, the totality and quality of the residual luster, and the surfaces' condition. They all have their particular influences on the overall coin grade.

Grading is a hard task made more complex by the need to be thorough in examining all contributing factors. And because the judgment is made by a human, there is bound to be differences of opinion and, thus, differences in grade that a coin may receive.

C. Proof Coins

Proof coins are those that have never been placed in general circulation. They were minted using specially polished and treated dies. Whereas coins minted for ordinary daily use are struck only once, proof coins are struck twice or more to create a highly detailed mirrored surface. By striking the coin more than once, the metal is forced into all the crevices of the die. This produces a very fine detail to the coin's image. This fine detail does not usually appear on Non-proof coins. Proof coins are usually sold at higher premium prices because of the extra labor and higher production cost.

Presidential Coins Proof Set

Grading of proofs is similar to the grades used for uncirculated coins using PR 60 to PR 70. PR 70 is rare or nonexistent if some cases. A proof coin can be mishandled or show wear because of cleaning. This fact can lower the grade of the coin below PR 60. Proof coins can show tarnishing or darkening too, just like uncirculated coins.

D. Split Grades.

A split grade is given to a coin when significant differences exist between the obverse and the reverse sides. This grade is denoted with a "/".Normally, the coin's overall grade is determined by its worst side. Again, an intermediate value may be given when the difference is significant, particularly if the reverse is lower. For example, a coin with a grade of MS 60/61 would have an overall grade of MS 60, and another coin with MS 65/63 would have an overall grade of MS 64.

Where Can you Find Coins?

Finding Rare and Collectible Coins

For many people, coin collecting began as a hobby. Nonetheless, you can hear other people say (or you have most likely heard yourself) about the news of people cashing in on their old coins. This prompted additional people to embark on a coin-collecting spree. If you want to start collecting coins, there are various places to start.

Coin Stores

Several store owners are dealers who know a lot about coins and sell some of them as well. These coin shops are an excellent place to learn more about coins and coin collecting. These coin shops may be pricey since they are looking to sell their coins for a profit. You can receive great rates for your coins if you have enough knowledge and/or have someone who knows a lot about coin collecting on your side.

Coin Displays

There will be occasions when your local mall features a display from a number of coin vendors. These will allow you to view their collection and purchase a couple of them for a lesser price due to competition. You will most likely also find several brand-new coins that are available for purchase and would be excellent additions to your collection.

These coin displays are wonderful for buyers and coin collectors who want to see rare and difficult-to-find coins.

Websites/Mail Orders

There are numerous dealers worldwide, and most of them have websites where you may pay them by mail order or any online payment method such as PayPal. You should conduct your homework on these companies and properly study their rules to ensure that you can get your money back if you have problems with the coin you purchased.

There are most certainly a slew of fraudulent websites vying for your money for every real website. Before paying anybody online, you should solicit feedback and avoid disclosing any passwords or P.I.N.s.

Markets on the cheap

This type of site is an unexpected place to find rare coins. Nonetheless, these areas have different pricing perceptions due to their lack of awareness of how a coin is priced. You will come across expensive coins, but if you are lucky, you may come across an unusual coin somewhere in those piles of coins, which will make it worthwhile for you to search.

Sellers in flea markets are usually looking for a quick sale and would most likely offer you a discount if you buy their items in quantity. Try to purchase additional items and have your coin added as a bonus.

Auctions

If you want to invest in really rare coins, the best place to go is to an auction. Auctions are the only places where you may find people selling their rarest and most expensive coins.

Many of these auctions are taking place online, and the majority of the sellers are looking for the highest bidders. However, you should be aware that some of these merchants are scammers and will not make the amount you pay worthwhile. Before you try to acquire one from an online auction, you should learn more about these coins and how much they are worth.

Coin Collectors from Other Countries

Coin collectors frequently have duplicate coins that they want to sell at a lower price than the market price. The only problem is that finding another coin collector like you is tough. Online groups, forums, and (if you have one) local groups are the greatest places to look. Other coin collectors are the ideal people to approach if you want to start your collection. They can offer you recommendations, discounts, and some may even be attracted to give you a few of their coins to start your collection.

Coin collecting is an investment, just like any other. They depreciate, whereas other coins may have an upward trend. The most effective way to benefit from coin collecting is to keep up with the latest news and coin values. These will not only help you avoid being duped by various sellers but will also teach you how to price a coin without a catalog.

Identifying And Avoiding Counterfeit Coins

Counterfeit and altered coins are more than an annoyance; they are fraudulent coins that detract from the hobby of coin collecting. They betray our faith in the currency and in one another. They detract from the enjoyment of the hobby. Buyers lose tens of thousands of dollars every year when they unwittingly acquire counterfeit or altered coins.

Every day, someone in the country purchases a counterfeit coin without realizing it. Unfortunately, the individual selling the currency is frequently ignorant that they are dealing with a counterfeit or changed coin.

It is a federal offense to counterfeit or modifies a real coin to improve its numismatic value. However, this does not deter the low-life thieves who continue to produce thousands of counterfeit and altered coins each year.

There are websites where you may purchase counterfeit coins of almost any denomination ever made by the United States Mint. The majority of these sites are hosted in Asia, where copyright, patents, and trademarks are routinely ignored and infringed.

While the federal government is aware of the issue, few actions are in place to deter violators. It is your responsibility to understand the coin you purchase and protect your investment.

What exactly is a counterfeit coin?

A counterfeit coin was created to look like a genuine coin.

What exactly is a tampered coin?

An altered coin is a standard coin that has been changed by adding or subtracting metal in order to imitate a scarce or expensive numismatic coin.

Crooks have gotten better at making false coins over the years. As technology has advanced, so have the manufacturing procedures used to produce counterfeit coins. I am aware that counterfeit coins are being produced in the same manner as genuine ones in one situation. The counterfeiters are brave, or dumb, enough to photograph their minting procedure and post it online.

The issue isn't confined to high-value numismatic coins. Any coin with a high enough value has been counterfeited. Recently, counterfeited $1 American Silver Eagle bullion coins were discovered in the United States. They were of such high quality that even coin specialists were taken in when they first saw them.

So, how can you safeguard yourself, your money, and your hobby?

Fortunately, counterfeit coin detection equipment is widely accessible and simple to use. The finest tools to utilize are your eyes and intellect, for the most part.

How to Spot Fake and Alternate Coins

1. Suppose it appears to be too good to be true. Most valuable coins will trade for close to their face value in the coin world. The only exclusions would be coins that the vendor does not know of. That will be uncommon, though, because most individuals understand how to calculate the worth of a coin.

   Be wary of coins that are only a few pennies on the dollar. If you are presented with a rare coin that you know is worth several thousand dollars and the vendor is just asking a few dollars for it, it is most likely a forgery. Buy no coin from a merchant that does not offer a suitable return policy. Most genuine dealers have a policy that permits you to return a coin after you've inspected it and discovered flaws.

2. Understand the coin you're interested in. Before purchasing any high-value coin, do your homework.

Look for images of authentic coins and analyze both the obverse and reverse. Learn everything there is to know about the coin, including current market values. Compare the coin you want to buy to recognized authentic coins or high-resolution images of that coin.

3. An associate of a friend once provided me with a Morgan silver dollar to purchase. It was a lovely mint state coin! So, why didn't I purchase it? It was a forgery. The Branch Mint where it was purportedly hit produced no Morgan dollars that year. The coin did not exist. That isn't the first time I've seen such fake coins. That's why it's critical to understand everything there is to know about the coin you're considering purchasing.

This is especially true with changed coins. The term "altered coins" refers to coins that look like something they are not. The 1916-D Mercury Dime is a good example.

Coin doctors take a plain Philadelphia-minted dime with no mint stamp and glue a "D" mintmark. Examining the coin with a magnifying glass shows the deceptive approach.

Coins that have been certified. When purchasing high-value coins, consider acquiring only coins certified by one of the three major third-party grading companies, PCGS, NGC, or ANACS. Coins encased by any other firm are suspicious. The initial stage for PCGS, NGC, or ANACS is to determine the authenticity of a coin. Always go ahead and double-check that the slabbed coin you're interested in is the same coin encapsulated by PCGS, NGC, or ANACS. Counterfeit slabs from these grading businesses have been identified. Each of the three firms listed above has internet databases with images of the validated coins. Check the coin you wish to acquire against that internet database to guarantee it is the same coin.

Counterfeit Coins Must Be Tested

1. Use a strong magnet to test the coin. The United States Mint has only made one magnetic coin. That was the 1943 Lincoln Cent, which was fashioned of steel planchets. The majority of China's counterfeit coins are fabricated with iron-based planchets. It is a forgery if any US-minted coin you test is even marginally attracted to the magnet.

2. Determine the weight of the coin. All coins manufactured by the United States Mint have a known weight and will fluctuate in weight by less than 1%. Make sure you purchase a scale that can weigh down to the tenth of a gram. Diet scales are insufficiently accurate. Place the coin on the scale and compare its weight to the coin's listed weight. Do not purchase that coin if it changes by more than 1% above or below the stated weight.

3. Measure the coin. Measure the diameter of the coin with a small-scale caliper. The diameter of all US-minted

coins is a known fact. If the measurement differs by more than 1%, the coin is most likely counterfeit.

4. Examine the coin's surfaces. Examine the coin using an 8X-10X magnifying. If the coin seems bumpy or bubbly, it is likely to be a forgery. These signs are often seen on coins made of poured metals. Examine the coin's edge for seams in the metal, which would indicate pouring. All U.S. coins with a denomination greater than 5 cents have reeded edges. If the reeds are uneven or absent, you should think that the coin is a forgery.

5. Keep a handy reference of U.S. coinage on hand. The Redbook U.S. Coin reference series comes highly recommended by me. Almost every coin shop I've ever visited has these in stock. Stop in, meet the dealer, see his coin collection, and get the current copy. They may also be found on Amazon. Every coin manufactured by the United States Mint is covered, as are the weight and dimension of

those pieces. Get one, put it on your desk, and consult it whenever you have a coin-related question.

When acquiring high-value things, there will always be hazards. That applies to everything. You may find counterfeits of almost every popular product you can think of in the marketplace. Guitars, blenders, trousers, handbags, and even automobiles have all been counterfeited.

Before you hand over your money, be sure you know what you're getting.

This guide will not detect every counterfeit or tampered coin. It will identify the obvious flaws. Counterfeiters have become increasingly skilled at their evil trade. Well-made counterfeit coins have duped even professionals in the subject on occasion.

You may reduce that danger by being aware of your currencies and being proactive in testing the coins you're thinking about buying. You will come across counterfeit coins and coins that have been changed to look to be something they are not at some time in your coin collecting career. Prepare ahead of time. It's your best line of defense.

Conclusion

People collect coins for a variety of reasons. Some collectors are drawn to the pastime because they are interested in its history. Each coin depicts a snapshot of people's daily life from decades, if not centuries, past. These coins were held in the hands of thousands of people, some of whom you may have heard about.

Studying the subject and seeking out new information as it becomes available are essential steps toward being a great coin collector. Join a local coin club if one exists in your region.

Look for coin collecting clubs on the internet. This might be a great networking opportunity for you, as well as a chance to meet someone who has the coin you're seeking for. The more coin collectors you know, the more opportunities you'll have to add to your collection while generating money.

Printed in Great Britain
by Amazon